## CONTENTS

Welcome ..................................................................... 2

Forgiveness—Who Needs It?—An Introduction ..................... 3

Is It My Turn to Lead? .................................................. 5

Racing the Clock ......................................................... 7

When Faith Crossings Happen ........................................ 9

Article: "Teach Your Children about a Forgiving God" ........... 10

Session Schedule ........................................................ 12

About FAITH CROSSINGS ........................................... 13

Session 1:  Do I Need Forgiveness? ................................. 14

Session 2:  Why Must I Forgive Others? ........................... 26

Session 3:  How Do I Forgive? ...................................... 36

Session 4:  How Many Times Must I Forgive? ................... 46

Session 5:  Must We *Always* Forgive? ........................... 54

Session 6:  Does Forgiveness Involve More than Just Me
and the Other Person? ................................................ 64

Enriching the Experience ............................................. 76

---

Published by Christian Board of Publication, St. Louis, Missouri
Writers: Myrna A. Phillips     Art Director: Michael A. Domínguez
and Noel Phillips              Cover design: Michael Foley
Series Editor: Michael E. Dixon    Cover art: Elaine Young
Interior design: Arista Graphics and Elizabeth Wright

© 1999 Christian Board of Publication, St. Louis, Mo. All rights reserved. No part of this publication may be reproduced without the publisher's permission.

All scripture quotations are from the *New Revised Standard Version Bible*, copyright 1989 by the Division of Christian Education of the National Council of Churches of Christ in the USA. In some instances, adaptations may have been made for the sake of inclusive language and clarity. Used by permission.

Printed in the United States of America.
Visit our Web site: www.cbp21.com

# WELCOME TO FORGIVENESS—WHO NEEDS IT?

**IF...**

You are saying, "Help! I'm a leader! What do I do next?" go to pages 5–8.

You want to read an article that will help you as a parent, grandparent, or teacher of children, try "Teach Your Children about a Forgiving God" on pages 10–11.

You want to find out more about the series as a whole, turn to "About FAITH CROSSINGS" on page 13.

You're getting ready for the first meeting of your FAITH CROSSINGS group and want to read Session 1 before you get there (always a good idea), it begins on page 14.

You want to discover unique activities to add to your FAITH CROSSINGS experience, check out "Enriching the Experience" on page 76.

You want to discover current and upcoming FAITH CROSSINGS titles, see page 80.

You want to find out more about Christian Board of Publication or place an order, call us at 1-800-366-3383 or visit our Web site at www.cbp21.com.

You want to send us questions about this course or the series, e-mail us at curriculm@cbp21.com, or write us at FAITH CROSSINGS, Christian Board of Publication, P.O. Box 179, St. Louis, M0 63166.

# FORGIVENESS—
# WHO NEEDS IT?
## AN INTRODUCTION

Forgiveness plays a key role in our relationships. From the beginning of time it has provided a means to mend broken relationships, maintain daily interactions, and bring peace to the end of devastating events. Forgiveness touches our lives personally, in community, and across society. It can take place in an encounter at the grocery store or at the peace talks in the Middle East. However, above all, forgiveness is a journey modeled by God. We see its path in the scriptures from the first incident of humanity's disobedience in the garden of Eden through Jesus Christ on the cross in the New Testament. Forgiveness is a critical concept for us to understand and practice in our faith journeys as Christians.

Forgiveness is a complex topic, and one that is deeply personal. In this study, you will have the chance to explore the scriptures about forgiveness and discern how the scriptures apply to daily living. The journey of forgiveness is a process that may happen quickly or may develop over months or years. Understanding the process gives permission to use the time needed, so that when forgiveness takes place it is authentic. When that happens, peace replaces pain. Frequently we forget that forgiveness is what happens toward the completion of the process. It is not appropriate to start the process with forgiveness and then try to work it through.

Personal safety is crucial to this study. In order to really understand the journey of forgiveness, members of the group will be asked to share their own experiences if they choose. A safe environment is essential to this type of disclosure, and confidentiality must be absolute and non-negotiable. Group members need to feel accepted without criticism, understood without probing, and cared for without being patronized. Creating such a climate in your group is not just the role of the leader, but of each and every group member. Interestingly, these are also conditions that support an environment of forgiveness.

One way to view the interactions within the group is to consider the difference between thoughts and feelings. Thoughts tend to come from our head, they may take time to form, they can involve one word or a whole dictionary of words, and they are arguable. People have differences of opinion, viewpoint, and understanding. Discussing these differences can be energizing and promote growth. Grappling with differences of opinion broadens our horizons.

Feelings are an animal of a different color. Feelings tend to come from our stomach or heart, they are usually immediate and spontaneous, and they can usually be expressed in one word, two at the most. What a person feels is non negotiable. To say to a person who is upset, "You shouldn't feel that way," or "Don't be upset," invalidates the person's experience and dismantles that person's trust. Being aware of whether a person is expressing thoughts or feelings enables the group to share together in ways that encourage health, trust, safety and self-awareness.

In looking at the journey of forgiveness, we often have the natural tendency to place blame. This tendency can result in assigning who is right and who is wrong so as to identify which party is to offer the forgiveness, so all parties can feel better. This is a common pattern but rarely helpful. There are times when there is no doubt that one person is an innocent victim totally blameless, and the other person(s) involved is totally accountable for inappropriate or viciously cruel behavior.

On the other hand, forgiveness frequently involves gray areas where all the people involved have participated intentionally or unintentionally in some way to create the problem. The majority of forgiveness issues are in the gray areas that mean the authentic, honest working through the journey of forgiveness is crucial.

We intentionally avoid using the term "victim" in this study, except in areas where the accountability is clearly one-sided. Plus, identifying another person (or one's self) as a victim can block the process of forgiveness, because it assigns blame and powerlessness. Being careful about semantics when discussing forgiveness provides an environment of openness and nonjudgmental opportunities for growth.

This study will not answer all the questions about forgiveness. Nor will it provide simple solutions for giving and receiving forgiveness. This study will offer a variety of ways to view forgiveness and encourage people to consider a broader picture of forgiveness. If this study raises more questions, challenges new thinking, and deepens spirituality, then it has served well.

# IS IT MY TURN TO LEAD?

By Cathy Myers Wirt

**Remember these leadership tips:**

- ✓ **Read** the session plan more than once before leading it.
- ✓ Allow enough time to **gather materials or resources** you may need.
- ✓ **Pray** for each group member by name during the week.
- ✓ Create a **spirit of hospitality and welcome** in the meeting space through decoration, refreshments (if appropriate to your time), and name tags if needed.
- ✓ Offer brief gathering times for quick **sharing of news** of the congregation/group.
- ✓ If sensitive topics arise, agree on a policy of **confidentiality.** Stories told in a group should be shared outside the group only when permission has been given.
- ✓ **Take all questions seriously** as a sign of the respect we hold for one another.
- ✓ If a person in the group has had a **tragedy** during the week, take time to deal with it even if it means delaying the session.
- ✓ **Direct** persons with serious emotional or spiritual dilemmas to the pastor.
- ✓ **Call persons who are absent** from the group during the week to check in on them and let them know that they have been missed.
- ✓ Encourage group members to **invite new people** to the group.
- ✓ **Ask for help** when you come across a topic or a problem in a group. You don't have to do this alone!
- ✓ **Allow silence** in the group while people think. Don't jump in too quickly to fill the quiet.
- ✓ Start and end the group with a **time of prayer.**
- ✓ Begin and end the session **on time.**
- ✓ **Vary your leading style** between thoughtful discussion, activity, and visual/auditory experiences. People learn in different ways.

- ✓ Connect the life of the group to the **congregation and the wider church.**
- ✓ **Watch the news media** for examples of the topics you are studying and bring in the articles for discussion and prayer.
- ✓ **Thank God** for the learning you are enjoying by leading the group. Leadership is one of the best ways to learn and to increase your own faith.
- ✓ **Don't assume** that the people in the room know one another well.
- ✓ **Don't argue.** When strongly different opinions are expressed, try to avoid a win/lose style of discussion.
- ✓ **Invite but don't coerce people to discuss.** Some people learn by listening and may be fully attentive without speaking.
- ✓ Help keep one person from **monopolizing the discussion.** Pass the discussion to another person by saying, "[name], what do you think about this idea/story?" Try always to do this in love.
- ✓ **Avoid getting sidetracked** by talking about people not in the room. Try to keep the discussion about the experiences and ideas of those in the room.
- ✓ **Avoid becoming unfocused** on the session. A group that has spun into other topics can be brought back by statements like "What in the session reminded you of that?" or "Wow, how did we get to this topic from today's session?" or "What you just said reminded me about our study today because…"

# RACING THE CLOCK
## A Leader's Guide to Getting through a Session

A typical FAITH CROSSINGS session gives more activities than time may allow. That's good news—there's a lot to choose from; and bad news—how do you choose? That depends. When you're leading a group of adults, there are a lot of variables! An activity that may take five minutes for one group may lead to a twenty-minute discussion in another. With all that in mind, here are some suggestions.

- Encourage everyone to read Before the Session before arriving. This section provides continuity and background to help the group members start "on the same page." Then the leader doesn't have to take time to summarize the information.
- In most cases, each session has four basic movements, each beginning with the phrase "Connecting with…" Be sure that you spend some time with each movement. (See the paragraph below on how to adapt this flow to a forty-five minute church school session.)
- Note the key activities. This logo after the title of an activity is your clue that it is essential to the session. If you don't have enough time to cover everything, be sure you cover the key activities.
- Pick and choose from the remaining activities, according to your interests and the interests of the group. If your group doesn't like an arts-based activity, for example, that may be a good one to draw a big X through before the session even begins.
- Go with the flow. Don't let agenda anxiety put a premature end to a really great discussion. And don't drag out an activity that people aren't responding to—just summarize and move on.

### Adapting to a church school setting

Each session is written for a ninety-minute group setting. If you want to use it in church school, how do you adapt? Two suggestions:

1. Allow twelve weeks for the six sessions. During the first week of a given session, cover what you can and close with a prayer. When the next week's session begins, summarize what the group covered the first week. Then work through the remaining activities.

2. Lead one session a week for six weeks. If you do this, there will probably be time for little more than the key activities. Highlight some of the important discussion questions you wish to include from the other activities. Encourage the group members to read the whole session, but select those activities for group use that connect to your particular group.

# WHEN FAITH CROSSINGS HAPPEN

Our life experiences and our faith often cross paths. We come to moments when we need our faith to help us interpret the meaning of our life experiences and to make Christian choices. Or our life experiences cause us to rethink our beliefs. When we come to such crossing points between faith and daily life, our lives change.

**Faith crossings happen when people share their beliefs lovingly and honestly, in a context of faith and love.** The way other people live out and express their faith shapes our own. A Christian, small group setting creates a context for this to happen. We become pilgrims together on a faith journey. Every FAITH CROSSINGS session promotes this interaction with activities under this heading and icon: **Connecting with one another.**

**Faith crossings happen when we open ourselves to new discoveries about life and faith.** Whether it's in reading the Bible or the daily news, downloading from the Internet or watching television, we receive new information that helps shape our understanding. Every FAITH CROSSINGS session promotes new learning with activities under this heading and icon: **Connecting with the theme.**

**Faith crossings happen when we decide what to do next.** How do our faith and experiences lead us to change the course of our daily lives? Toward what actions do our faith crossings prod us? Every FAITH CROSSINGS session promotes this decision making with activities under this heading and icon: **Connecting with life.**

**Faith crossings happen when we celebrate God's presence in our midst.** God calls us to respond, to praise, to pray, to worship, to love. Every FAITH CROSSINGS session promotes worship and reflection with activities under this heading and icon: **Connecting with God.**

# TEACH YOUR CHILDREN ABOUT A FORGIVING GOD[1]

By Delia Halverson

Sometimes we think that directing our child's every move so that he or she doesn't make any mistakes is an act of kindness. Actually, it is important for children to learn from mistakes along the way. Unless they learn to acknowledge their mistakes, they will never learn to ask for forgiveness.

Saying "I'm sorry" and asking for forgiveness is more than lip service. It must come from the heart, and there must be a true desire to change. Our word *repentance* goes further than saying, "I'm sorry." To repent is to turn around—to redirect life in a new direction.

In Jesus' prayer example he did not say, "Forgive us our debts *because* we forgive" but "*as* we forgive." God forgives us even before we ask, but nonetheless we must ask. This is the example of forgiveness that we must pattern. Our forgiveness should not hinge on being asked, but rather we should give that forgiveness in our hearts even before the asking, and then the person only needs to accept our forgiveness.

Work with some of these experiences with your children.

• Read the book *Love You Forever* by Robert Munsch and Sheila McGraw (Firefly Books, 1986). In the story the child spends his day pulling books off shelves and things out of the refrigerator. He even flushes his mother's watch down the toilet. The mother feels he is driving her crazy. But after he is asleep at night she holds him and sings, "I'll love you forever, I'll like you for always; so long as I'm living, my baby you'll be" (page 3). This book does not have a religious word in it, but does lay a religious foundation.

• Offer your child choices appropriate for his or her age. Choices should broaden, instead of narrow, as children get older. Young children can make choices between several options. With experience, they learn to create their own options.

• When you must voice disapproval, assure the child that your love continues.

• Sibling rivalry is normal. Use these opportunities to allow children to work through their own problems. Ask them to work together to write an agreed-upon account of just what happened.

- Elementary children are into fairness. Following the rules is a part of their developmental stage. Help them realize that God forgives out of love, not out of our deserving it.
- Elementary children and teens can appreciate Jesus' forgiveness for those who killed him. Read the scripture passage, Luke 23:34.

---

[1]Delia Halverson, *How Do Your Children Grow?* (Chalice Press, 1999), 32–33. Used by permission.

# SESSION SCHEDULE

### Session 1
When _____ Leader _____
Where _____

### Session 2
When _____ Leader _____
Where _____

### Session 3
When _____ Leader _____
Where _____

### Session 4
When _____ Leader _____
Where _____

### Session 5
When _____ Leader _____
Where _____

### Session 6
When _____ Leader _____
Where _____

### Special Activities
When _____ Leader _____
Where _____

# ABOUT FAITH CROSSINGS

*"I searched for you, and searched for you, until you found me."*
*—Augustine, an early Christian theologian, in a prayer to God*

Faith is not a static condition, something that keeps us tied down to a certain outlook. Instead, it is a companion on a journey, a great search for God. We discover that the God we search for is the God who is with us as we travel through the years of our lives.

For the Christian, faith crossings are not taken alone, not even alone with God. Ours is a faith born in community. We learn and grow from one another. Our guide on our faith travels, Jesus Christ, points out that loving God and loving our neighbor cannot be separated from each other. We need one another for support and guidance along life's road.

Faith in the God of Jesus Christ sometimes lifts us to another, spiritual realm. More often, it helps us see God's presence in the ordinary. Joseph F. Schmidt reminds us of this in his book *Praying Our Experiences* (St. Mary's Press, 1980, 52–53).

> An experience of beauty or joy or a moment of intimacy may also put us in touch with an awareness of God's love and blessing. We ride on a mountain road, or walk along a beach, or experience the affection and complete acceptance of a friend, and we suddenly awake to the realization that at work in our life is a force of love and care that fully encompasses us and all of reality. We see more clearly that we are loved quite undeservedly not just by a friend but by Life. We become more aware that we and all creation are being sustained and nourished by a beneficent free Love. And in this we realize God's word uttered in blessing and care.

As we travel together in faith, we learn what love is all about. FAITH CROSSINGS, a series of small group resources, is designed to bring adult Christians together for

- ▲ mutual growth in faith, love, and knowledge
- ▲ mutual support and fellowship, and
- ▲ deepening relationship with God, Christ, and the church

so that they may

- ▲ connect the Christian faith with their everyday lives, and
- ▲ live lives of active discipleship and faithful witness.

# Do I Need Forgiveness?

*Session Focus: The road to forgiveness begins with the reality of our own individual humanness. How does our humanness relate to the need for forgiveness? What is sin and why do I need to recognize ways in which I sin? Is it possible to have a healthy personal life and not ask for or receive forgiveness? What is God's attitude towards me?*

Scripture Used: Psalm 51; Psalm 103; Romans 3:21–26.

**BEFORE THE SESSION**

Reflect on what forgiveness means to you.

Within each person is the capacity to sin. As humans we make mistakes. Every relationship brings with it tensions and challenges. Within human interaction there is always the possibility of suffering, inflicting injury, and hurt feelings. Conflicts exist in every community regardless of how small or large. It is inevitable that human beings will have tension and conflict. The question is not whether there will be injury. Rather, the real question is: How will we choose to handle hurt, injury, alienation, and tension?

The ability to feel is at the very core of who we are as human beings. God created us to have feelings, and Jesus modeled the need for feelings in our lives. The feelings of hurt, anger, confusion, and pain alert us that something is wrong (not unlike how the pain

Review together appropriate portions of the course introduction (p. 3) and "Is It My Turn to Lead?" (p. 5) to guide the discussion on establishing ground rules. When the group agrees upon its ground rules, write them on a sheet of newsprint and post it for all to see, or have individual group members write them on a blank page of their books.

Discuss.

Read and reflect, either as a total group, or smaller groups.

in a tooth alerts us that we need to see a dentist). The responsibility, then, is to choose how to respond and act on feelings in ways that are responsible and facilitate healing.

## 1. Meet one another and establish ground rules

Take a few moments for introductions. If you are comfortable in so doing, tell about why you joined this group and what your expectations are. Note that "Forgiveness—Who Needs It?" is a course that attempts to understand biblical teachings about forgiveness and apply them to our daily lives. It is not a therapy group. We do hope, however, that deep and honest discussions of this theme will help the group members grow as individuals and will draw the group closer together.

For this to happen, and to avoid broken trust, you need ground rules. Here are some to consider: Respect confidentiality. Nothing said in the group goes outside the group without permission. Be sensitive to each person's right to speak only for his or her self. We can choose (or not) to share our stories. It is inappropriate to share the story of another person without previous permission. Respect a person's right to not discuss or respond to a question.

## 2. Define terms

We are going to consider two different dimensions to forgiveness. One involves our relationship with God. The other involves our relationship with others and ourselves.

When we consider our relationship to God, we see forgiveness in relationship to sin. What is sin? How were you taught what sin is? Who taught you? What is your earliest memory of hearing about sin? Is sin a serious issue? If so, what makes sin a life matter that we need to address?

*Do I Need Forgiveness?*

The word "forgiveness" brings to each person a multitude of definitions based on each person's life experiences. Reflect on the definition of forgiveness, as you understand it. If you were to define forgiveness in one clear sentence, what would that be?

As a whole group, work together to blend your thoughts and feelings to define forgiveness. Use a consensus process. Write on newsprint (or chalkboard) a clear statement (a sentence or paragraph) of how this group defines or identifies forgiveness. Post this statement where it can be seen, and to which members may refer during the weeks of the study of this topic.

Sin is that which separates us from God, others, and ourselves. Sin is problematic because it is a block that prevents openness, honesty, and authentic interaction in relationships. Sin can be a block to our being all that God calls us to be. Discuss in the group ways in which sin is a block.

3. **Contrast real versus imagined guilt**

Frequently people become confused about the differences between real guilt and imagined guilt. Guilt is the feeling we experience when we have, in fact, done something wrong or know we omitted doing something, and this choice caused injury. Sometimes we are totally aware of this guilt. At other times, however, the feeling of guilt may be hidden from conscious awareness, more like a nagging feeling or sense of discomfort that bothers us. Real guilt calls us to repent, make amends, and commit to changing our behavior.

An interesting twist is that sometimes we feel what we believe is guilt when, in fact, we have not committed a wrong. Frequently we label what we feel as guilt when actually we harbor a resentment that we are not acknowledging or facing. This confusion seems especially prevalent in families, since our culture does not encourage anger in women but does affirm women who feel guilty. Most males do not verbalize regularly, "I feel so guilty…I was late, I did not mow the lawn, I forgot to make that phone call, etc." Women in our society frequently feel anger but identify the feelings as guilt as a matter of habit. People who tend to accept responsibility for others and/or have poor emotional boundaries also will struggle to define real versus imagined guilt.

*Discuss.*

In order to accept responsibility for one's sin or guilt, it is helpful to determine when we are experiencing real guilt or imagined guilt. Discuss and evaluate which of these examples illustrate real guilt and which illustrate imagined guilt. Which of these examples may be about unexamined resentment? What are some other examples from your life about real or imagined guilt?

"I feel so guilty because…:

- "I promised I would not tell my friend's secret, and I just blurted it out."
- "My brother needs help on his house this weekend, and I already have another commitment."
- "Other people's children seem well behaved and mine become wiggly and distracting in church."
- "I took office supplies from my work site without permission."
- "My parents are unhappy and I cannot seem to make it better."
- "I cannot seem to get my act together."

The whole issue about how I need forgiveness is fundamentally about honesty. I need to be honest about my guilt, whether real or imagined. Perhaps I focus on imagined guilt because it distracts me from facing my real guilt. Is that a possibility? What do I gain by refusing to admit I have sinned?

In order to better identify guilt, let us remember the difference between guilt and shame. In over-simplified terms, guilt is when we have *made* a mistake; shame is when we feel that we *are* a mistake. Some people have been told (especially as children) that there is something inherently wrong with them, that their personhood is a mistake. When this happens, they may feel vivid shame almost all the time regardless of the situation. Therefore, if such people make a mistake because they are human, what they may feel is shame, because they believe that *who* they are is wrong, not *what* they did is wrong. How might shame cloud our ability to accept accountability for everyday mistakes we make? How might this intensity of shame shape how a person gives and receives love? gives and receives forgiveness?

### 4. Explore the importance of ritual

People by their very nature grow and learn by process. We have a need to authenticate our feelings, to perform rituals around important life issues. A couple may validate their relationship and commitment to each other by vowing in the presence of others to be faithful to one another. Graduation ceremonies and the receiving of a diploma mark the concrete closure of an educational process. Baptism is an outward act expressing a changed relationship with God. Traditions at holiday times are rituals that express our thoughts and feelings about the meaning of the holiday and about our families.

What are ways you can identify that people have expressed their feelings in concrete ways? in ways of rituals? How is this process helpful in bringing closure or a sense of completion? Name a family event that is actually a ritual and explain how this came to be. Name a ritual of your congregation; explain how this came to be. The process of forgiveness can be acted out in a ritual, such as a group confession of sin and words of assurance in a worship service. What other instances can you think of where ritual, formal or informal, helps forgiveness happen? (For example, a parent and child may always hug and make up after the consequences of a disciplinary problem.)

## 5. Consider how secrets block forgiveness

Secrets block the process of healing and prohibit the ritual of forgiveness. Secrets influence and define a person, create dysfunction in families, and can cause physical as well as spiritual illness. Mental health professionals usually believe "we are as sick as the secrets we keep."

*Discuss.*

Do you agree that we are as sick as the secrets we keep? What is the difference between privacy and secrets? How does a family's pattern of protecting privacy or hiding secrets affect how the family forgives? What happens in families where secrets are kept, perhaps for generations? How does it impact a congregation when a church confuses privacy and secrets? How does the inappropriate keeping of secrets affect how the process of forgiveness happens (or does not happen) in a church? How do secrets impact church rituals such as weddings, baptisms, funerals, dedication services, or even eucharist?

*Reflect on secrets and rituals.*

## 6. Explore the scriptures

*Form three teams and assign each one a passage to read and discuss: Psalm 51; Psalm 103; Romans 3:21–26.*

As you read your team's passage, make a list of the feelings the assigned scripture stirred in you. Rather than focus on the passage's content, focus on the feelings that the scripture invokes. Help your team compile a list on paper. Then the three teams will form one group again to share the feelings each team compiled.

Which feelings were similar? Which feelings were different? How did the three scriptures elicit feelings? Are these feelings ones that we experience on a daily basis? What does how we feel have to do with our need for forgiveness? How might a person express these feelings through already-established rituals or in developing new rituals?

*Do I Need Forgiveness?*

## 7. Study Old Testament understandings of sin and forgiveness

The biblical concepts of sin and forgiveness regarding God and God's laws as found in the Old Testament concern both human-with-divine and human-with-human relationships. Sin is any act or action that is contrary to God's law and that disrupts or causes a break in relationship. Sin is more than just bad behavior or an act or wrongdoing, it is a matter of the heart. Sin includes the prior contemplation, intention, temptation, and harboring of thoughts that lead to wrongful action or behavior. An outward act springs from an inward thought, desire, or feeling. Sin results in separation of humans from humans and humans from God. In the Old Testament the consequences of sin can be quite harsh. (See Joshua 24:19–20.)

Beginning with the Old Testament, forgiveness is the process required to restore a broken or disrupted relationship, be it between God and humans or humans with humans. The process of forgiveness in the Old Testament includes the realization/recognition of the wrongdoing (sin), repentance (accepting the responsibility and having a change of heart), and reaction (a sacrifice to symbolize a change in action or behavior). In Leviticus 4—6, the Old Testament concepts of sin, sacrifice, and forgiveness are explained in detail.

In the Old Testament, God's act of forgiveness takes several forms. Different Hebrew words are used to reflect different forgiving actions of God. The Hebrew word, *kaphar,* means "to cover" or "blot out," the idea being to cover a blemish. (See Psalm 51:1,9.) *Nasa* conveys the idea of "lifting up or away," removing the sin. (See Psalm 103:12.) And *salach* is used to give the sense of "letting go" or "sending away." (See Psalm 51:2,7.) These different actions by God to forgive are in correlation to the

---

**Discuss:** Create in one sentence your definition of sin. Is it the same or different than described here in the text? Share your definition with the group and discuss. Is one wrong act more sinful than another? to you? to God?

sins committed. Different sins call for different sacrifices and are treated by God accordingly.

## 8. Explore God's process of sacrifice and forgiveness

God is a loving and caring God who seeks to be in relationship with creation. Thus God provides the way to maintain the relationship with creation, even when it (we) go astray. God forgives. The psalmist knew this when writing, "Create in me a clean heart, O God, and put a new and right spirit within me" (Psalm 51:10).

The psalmist also knew the true nature of God as loving and forgiving,

> *But the steadfast love of the* LORD *is from everlasting to everlasting on those who fear him, and his righteousness to children's children, to those who keep his covenant and remember to do his commandments. (Psalm 103:17–18)*

God seeks to be in relationship, and establishes ways to maintain that relationship, through love, compassion, mercy, and forgiveness. God restores broken relationships through the process of forgiveness. In the New Testament the concept of forgiveness goes beyond the law. In Matthew 5:17ff, Jesus defines sin and righteousness not in terms of acts or behavior, but in terms of thoughts and desires, and what is our intent, and what is in our hearts. Jesus also, then, redefines forgiveness, not only by his words but also by his very being "the Lamb of God who takes away the sin of the world" (John 1:29). What stories can you recall where Jesus forgave someone?

The whole process of forgiveness, in both the Old and New Testaments, is one of salvation, making us one with God, keeping us in relationship. The Old Testament concept of forgiveness is fulfilled in Christ who becomes the sacrifice for sin, so that all

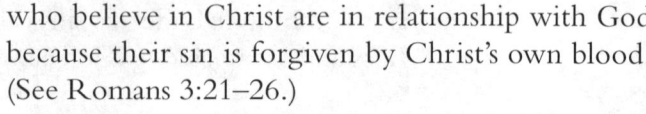

who believe in Christ are in relationship with God because their sin is forgiven by Christ's own blood. (See Romans 3:21–26.)

All of this can be summed up in the familiar scripture of John 3:16: "For God so loved the world that he gave his only son, so that everyone who believes in him may not perish but may have eternal life."

> Discuss the connection between sacrifice and forgiveness.

Have you forgiven someone in your life who wronged you? What process took place? Was there a sacrifice? by whom? to whom? Was God involved? What does John 3:16 mean to you personally? If someone asked you to explain the theology of forgiveness, how would you explain it in simple language?

### 9. Integrate the theology with your life

Forgiveness is both an easy subject and a most difficult subject. On the one hand, sermons are preached regularly about the theology of and the need for forgiveness. Forgiveness is a familiar topic. On the other hand, the difficulty comes when we honestly reflect on the times in our lives when we have sinned (or been sinned against) in ways that are life-changing. God calls us to forgive in authentic ways, not ways where there is denial, a covering up, a pretending, or a superficial truce. Authentic, restoring forgiveness is difficult.

Choose a partner. Take approximately fifteen minutes to complete this assignment, including discussion time with your partner.

> As a leader, be open by sharing with your partner.

Each person will reflect on the following questions, then decide who in the partnership will speak first. The first person will answer all the questions while the listener remains totally silent. Then the pair will switch roles. It is essential that the listener not speak, interrupt, or express their feelings while they are in the listening role. A reminder: Everything said is confidential to that pair.

Each person will take some quiet moments to reflect on a time when they have sinned. Choose an example to share with your partner. *Important:* You need *not* share the nature of the sin itself; rather, you will be sharing the *response* to the sin.

When each person is ready to begin, please share the following with your partner:
- At what point did you realize you had sinned? before you sinned? during? after? much later after you gained wisdom and maturity?
- How did the sin affect your relationship with God and others?
- How did this sin affect how you see yourself?
- What was the impact of this sin externally?
- What was the internal impact of this sin? What feelings did you have? How did your physical body respond?
- How did this sin and response to the sin clarify for you what sin and forgiveness means?

### 10. Forgive yourself

The letting go of our pain around our sins can be difficult and almost seem impossible. Only when we internalize the truth that God forgives us can we begin the process of learning to forgive ourselves. Often our own lack of self-esteem blocks our ability to forgive ourselves, to believe God loves us enough to forgive us. Beating ourselves up does not serve us well nor does it honor God. Honestly making amends can help facilitate our letting go of our guilt and shame.

If learning to forgive ourselves is a process, what do you see as some of the steps in the process? Can I forgive others and still refuse to forgive myself? Can I forgive myself and still refuse to forgive others? How can I internalize that God forgives me? If my mistake contributed to the death or injury of another person, is it possible to totally forgive myself? Is forgiving myself an essential part of God's plan?

Discuss.

*Do I Need Forgiveness?*

> Lead the group in this self-forgiveness prayer exercise. Invite the people to close their eyes and review the following instructions. Allow some time for reflection between the steps. Close with an Amen.

Naming to ourselves what it is that we find difficult to forgive in ourselves is one step toward self-forgiveness. Asking for God's help is another. Consider engaging in a symbolic act to help you toward forgiving yourself. Name to yourself an act, attitude, event, or the name of someone you have hurt. Using a finger of one hand as a pencil, write the word you have named on the palm of your other hand. Hold your hands together in prayer for a moment. As the leader directs, open your hands and hold them palm up. Ask God silently to help you learn to forgive yourself for what you have named. Pray for those who may have been hurt in the occasion that you have recalled. Ask God silently for God's Spirit to work within you that you may be able to accept God's forgiveness.

### 11. Create a new and right spirit

In closing, the leader will guide the prayer by stating each incomplete sentence followed by a prayer so that any group members may complete the sentence. The group will then pray the response together before proceeding to the next incomplete sentence.

*Shared response:* "Create in me a clean heart, O God, and put a new and right spirit within me" (Psalm 51:10).

> Set a mood for worship. Perhaps light a candle or play quiet music. Reflect quietly on what it means that "for where two or three are gathered in my name, I am there among them" Matthew 18:20.

- God, we thank you today for...*(Pause for group to share)*...Shared response.
- God, teach us today about...*(Pause for group to share)*...Shared response.
- God, fill our souls today with...*(Pause for group to share)*...Shared response.
- God, forgive us today for...*(Pause for group to share)*...Shared response.
- God, for this coming week, grant us...*(Pause for group to share)*...Shared response.

Amen.

# JOURNAL

## 2

# Why Must I Forgive Others?

*Session Focus: As one way of reflecting God's forgiveness to us, we strive to forgive others. Forgiveness like this takes place in a journey of feeling, interaction, and action.*

Scriptures Used: Matthew 6:9–15; 18:23–35

**BEFORE THE SESSION**

Reflect on the Lord's Prayer. How, where, and when did you first learn it? What new meanings have you found in it?

Christians around the world share in common not only many of the same beliefs, but also many of the same practices. A very common practice is the sharing of the Lord's Prayer in unison during worship. Included in the Lord's prayer as Jesus taught it in the Gospel of Matthew (6:9–13) is a verse about forgiveness. "And forgive us our debts, as we also forgive our debtors;…" (RSV). The Greek word used here for forgive is *aphiemi* which means to send, let off or away. In this case it is used to mean letting a person off the responsibility of a debt owed. Most Christians know the Lord's Prayer by heart and can recite it from rote memory during worship. However, do we actually hear what we are saying? Could we pray that prayer aloud in good conscience if we took those words seriously? Could we pray that prayer if we pondered those words' true meaning before we entered worship?

*Forgiveness—Who Needs It?*

If you will notice, this is the only phrase in the prayer where Jesus makes further comment (see Matthew 6:14–15). For Jesus it is clear that forgiveness is a critical aspect of our faith journey; God's forgiveness of us, our forgiveness of one another. Forgiveness is the way we heal our broken relationships and live in harmony and community. That takes more than a quick thought or retort, "I'm sorry," or a superficial, "It won't happen again." Forgiveness in the biblical sense is a process or journey with steps to forgiveness. To Jesus, our earthly relationships are important avenues to our relationship with the divine. In fact, if we read this passage literally, our forgiveness from God depends upon our willingness and ability to forgive one another! Forgiveness like this takes place on a journey of feeling, interaction, and action. Forgiveness happens in an atmosphere of openness and acceptance. God's forgiveness adds the element of sacrifice. God's forgiveness has taken the journey of feeling, interaction, and action.

## 1. Recall how you learned the Lord's Prayer

The Lord's Prayer frequently has been taught to children at an early age or perhaps the children have learned it simply by hearing it prayed in church regularly. It is common for children to beam with pride at having accomplished the task of memorizing it. However, this does not mean that they understand it.

Tell the group about your earliest memory of the Lord's Prayer. When did you learn it, who taught it to you, and what did you understand about this prayer? In one or two sentences describe what the Lord's Prayer means to you today. How does this prayer impact your life?

## 2. Identify the definition of forgiveness in the Lord's Prayer

Read Matthew 6:9–15, hearing the scripture from different biblical versions. Focus on verses 12, 14 and

15. Together discuss what this verse means. Then work together as a group to rephrase into one or two sentences what expresses the essence of this scripture. Write the group's response on newsprint or chalkboard and post it for all to see.

Consider and respond to the following questions:
- How can (or can't) I forgive others as readily, unconditionally, and freely as God forgives?
- Am I forgiven by God if I do not forgive others? Why or why not?
- If I am forgiven by God only in proportion to my willingness and ability to forgive, what does that say about how I am forgiven?
- Is it possible to forgive if we have never experienced forgiveness? Why or why not?
- How do I know if I have been forgiven by God?

Keep in mind that the Lord's Prayer falls within the section of scripture known as the Sermon on the Mount. It was a time for Jesus to teach his disciples. This prayer, and especially the phrase that is the focus of this study, is not an admonition, but a lesson. Jesus is not only teaching about human forgiveness but God's forgiveness. The phrase in the prayer, "forgive us our debts as we also forgive our debtors," is the reminder that we must ask for forgiveness. It is part of our relationship with God, our faith journey, and so it is a part of our relationship with others, our life journey. God's unconditional love and forgiveness become the Christian's model and standard of forgiveness.

Biblical forgiveness, as it is described here, functions on three levels. First, there is God's forgiveness of us. It is always available. It is dependent upon our recognizing our sin and asking God for forgiveness. It also calls for a change in our attitude and action. We are called to learn from our sin and not repeat it. However, we will be forgiven "seven times seventy." The second level is the forgiveness of others when

---

**Have different versions of the Bible available; also have newsprint and markers handy.**

**Share together as a group.**

we have hurt them. Once again, this calls for our response, to own up to our responsibility for the wrong and a willingness to change our behavior to renew the relationship and build the trust that has been broken. The third level is our forgiveness of others when we have been hurt. And as in the parable of the unforgiving servant (the focus of study in our next scripture selection), this level of forgiveness is just as crucial as the other two levels.

### 3. Revisit a familiar parable

CONNECTING WITH THE THEME

Explore the parable by role playing. You may want to ask people ahead of time to read the parable and play the parts.

Read Matthew 18:21–35. Role-play the parable two times. The first set of players will role-play the story as portrayed in the scripture. Volunteers from the group will play the parts from the Bible using their own words but adhering to the scripture story line. In processing the role-play the "actors" will share how they felt doing their part. Did they identify with the person they portrayed? Would they have felt more comfortable playing a different role? Why?

The second role-play will be done by three different participants. The volunteers will gather together and leave the room, if that is helpful. The "actors" have five minutes to create a situation that represents the meaning of this scripture in today's culture with today's language. The "actors" will then role-play the situation for the group. They will then share their feelings with the group about how it felt to play each role. Could they easily identify with the person they portrayed? Would another role have been more comfortable? Why? How did the team decide on the situation to portray? What other situations did they consider? What did the group learn from observing the two role-plays?

Share together.

### 4. Examine your definition of forgiveness

In the parable of the unforgiving servant, Jesus provides an example of the phrase from the Lord's Prayer, "forgive us our debts, as we also forgive our debtors." Jesus told this parable after being prompted by Peter's question, "Lord, how many times shall I forgive my brother when he sins against me? Up to seven times?" Jesus' answer steps beyond the law, "Seven times seventy!" That is the model of God's forgiveness. The king in the parable is in the first case willing to excuse or forget the whole debt owed by the servant. Will God not forgive me, if I refuse to forgive? What happens to me if I am not forgiven? in my relationship to others? to God? What does it feel like to not be forgiven? to not be forgiving? What does it take to be forgiven? to be forgiving?

## 5. Digging deeper into the parable

A modern parable tells of a father and son's relationship. The father, wanting the son to be responsible, took the son to their backyard where there was a big stump. He told his son that every time the son did a hurtful act that he was to come to the stump and hammer a nail into the stump. On the other hand, the son was to remove a nail every time he did an act or deed that was helpful. After some time the son returned to the father with this insight, "I can remove the nails, but they leave holes." The father told him that the holes serve as reminders of the hurtful acts. Hopefully, the holes as reminders will also encourage the son not to repeat his mistakes.

Perhaps this parable expresses one of the more painful aspects of making mistakes that we must face. When we hurt another person, we sometimes impact their life in such a way that life is never the same again. People will frequently have a conflict, serious mistakes are made, and then the request is made that we "go back to how things used to be." There are errors in thinking here. First, when serious mistakes are made and lives are changed, going back to how things used to be is unrealistic because life has been permanently altered. Secondly, the past

> Divide the members into group Psalm to study these verses. Invite them to share their conclusions with each other.

somehow brought the problems, so to go back to things as they were will ultimately only produce the same results.

The unforgiving servant did not display the same forgiving attitude as did the king. In our humanness we sometimes find forgiving another person is very difficult. We also find in some circumstances that others are not willing to readily forgive us. Frederick L. Keefe in his short story "The Brother," defines the unforgiving servant's attitude as "a hard rock of a man, full of unblinking devotion. Hope without heart, form without feeling." With that description of a person, would you care to be their friend, would it be possible to be their friend, and would they let you close enough to be their friend? What does compassion have to do with forgiveness? If God offers us compassion and understanding, can we do less for each other? How do we offer compassion and forgiveness when the result of the injury is that our life will never be the same again?

> Discuss.

## 6. Explore the meaning of forgiveness in the secular realm 🗝

Relationships are built on trust, compassion, caring, and interaction. Sometimes we choose our friends, and other times through circumstances beyond our control we have to deal with people not of our choosing. We all have places where we must be on the job, in public, at an event, or placed with others that are quite different from us in background, ethnicity, sexual orientation, gender, or religious belief. How does our understanding of forgiveness translate into our everyday world? In the world of business the term used for a wrong on the job site is "grievance." And in most job situations there is a procedure used when a grievance happens, a grievance procedure. In most situations, however, there are clear-cut rules about how this procedure is to take place. The best hoped-for result is to have both parties become friends in a relationship more wholesome than before the grievance. The least hoped-for outcome is to find a way for each party to grit their teeth and tolerate the situation without having to be friends or even like one another.

For Christians God's forgiveness and call to forgive adds the element of compassion. It steps beyond the grievance procedure to seek to heal the relationship in a way that brings wholeness, harmony, and community. A grievance procedure's goal is to provide a productive workplace. The goal of God's forgiveness is to provide healthy relationships with one another and God.

> You may want to have an example to use as a starter.

Brainstorm together incidences in the secular world where forgiveness would be difficult. The group may create hypothetical situations, or members of the group may share stories from their personal life if they choose. Pick three incidents and focus on the following questions as they pertain to each incident:

- How is this a situation about forgiveness?
- How might a Christian speak about forgiveness in this situation?
- What language would convey the sacredness of forgiveness?
- If we offer forgiveness, what is the risk of being stereotyped as "holier than thou"?
- How might a person handle being teased or ridiculed for their beliefs about forgiveness?

> Discuss together everyday life experiences.

In one of Ann Landers' newspaper columns was an interesting quote, "Resentment is when you let someone you despise live in your head rent-free." In our lives hurt, injustice, and wrongdoing will happen. It can come from all sides and all sorts of people, including our children, our spouses, our parents, our pastors, our friends, our neighbors, our coworkers, and even ourselves. How we forgive in those situations is a barometer as to how we honestly understand and feel God's forgiveness. The way we forgive and the way we feel forgiven are eternally linked in Christ's definition of forgiveness, "forgive us our debts, as we also forgive our debtors"; they coexist, side by side, one with the other.

### 7. Let go of pain, experience forgiveness

Use this exercise as a quiet time to close the session. Reread the scripture lessons for this session: Matthew 6:12; 18:21–35 and focus on what forgiveness means to you.

On the paper write down a situation or situations for which you need to forgive someone else. *No one else will see these sheets of paper!* You may write whatever you want. At the front of the room or as part of the circle you will need a table on which there is a lit candle and a large metal bowl or metal waste can. (You will also want a fire extinguisher handy.) When everyone has had time to complete their writing, each member may take their paper to the candle, light the paper, and let it be consumed by the fire. (You may also do this with a fire in the fireplace, etc.)

Return to your place in an attitude of prayer. When everyone is finished, reflect on God's forgiveness and your forgiveness. The fire has helped you let go.

### 8. Sing and pray together

Sing together "Kum Ba Yah," an African folk song calling for God's presence. Afterward, join hands, pray the Lord's Prayer together, and leave the room thoughtfully and prayerfully, knowing you are forgiven as you have forgiven others.

Provide each person a small sheet of paper and a pencil or pen. You may wish to light a candle during the last two activities to signify God's presence.

Maybe someone in the group can provide guitar, piano, or drum accompaniment.

*Why Must I Forgive Others?*

# Kum ba Yah

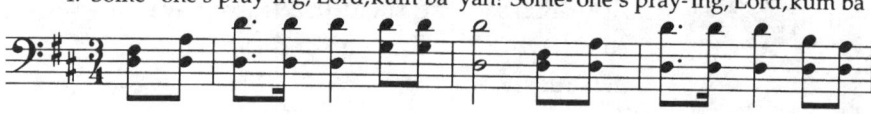

1. *Kum ba yah, my Lord, kum ba yah! Kum ba yah, my Lord, kum ba
2. Some-one's cry-ing, Lord, kum ba yah! Some-one's cry-ing, Lord, kum ba
3. Some-one's sing-ing, Lord, kum ba yah! Some-one's sing-ing, Lord, kum ba
4. Some-one's pray-ing, Lord, kum ba yah! Some-one's pray-ing, Lord, kum ba

yah! Kum ba yah, my Lord, kum ba yah! O Lord, kum ba yah!
yah! Some-one's cry-ing, Lord, kum ba yah! O Lord, kum ba yah!
yah! Some-one's sing-ing, Lord, kum ba yah! O Lord, kum ba yah!
yah! Some-one's pray-ing, Lord, kum ba yah! O Lord, kum ba yah!

*Come by here*
WORDS and MUSIC: Marvin Frey, 1938

DESMOND
88.85

*Forgiveness—Who Needs It?*

# JOURNAL

# 3

# How Do I Forgive?

*Session Focus: Is forgiveness supposed to be easy? If I am a Christian, will I be able to forgive others immediately just by telling myself I should? What part does reconciliation play in this journey of forgiveness?*

Scriptures Used: Genesis 33:1–17; 45:1–15; 50:15–21; Psalm 139:1–18

BEFORE THE SESSION

Read and reflect on the scriptures for this session.

The Old Testament story of Jacob and Esau has many twists and plots. Jacob, by trickery, obtained the blessing of his father, Isaac, that rightly belonged to Esau, the eldest son. This put much bitterness between the two brothers. The brothers parted for a long time. However, in Genesis 33:1–17, we see the two brothers reconciled. Jacob, in fear of his life, had the women and children of his family go before him when he saw Esau coming. It was Esau, who was wronged, that initiated the reconciliation. However, we also must note Jacob's repentant attitude. For forgiveness to have truly taken place in this story, a change of attitude had to come from both sides. There was the willingness to forgive and the desire to be forgiven. There was also an element of surprise. Jacob was surprised that Esau was willing to forgive him. He expected only retaliation, which was, by the cultural standards of the day, the proper consequence for Jacob's behavior. Jacob was also willing to make a sacrifice for the wrong he caused Esau. Esau at first refused, but then accepted. This is an intriguing model then, very early in the biblical account, of the journey of forgiveness. Notice the elements:

- the wrongful act
- the recognition of the wrongful act
- taking responsibility for that act
- the changing of attitudes
- a dialogue of repentance and forgiveness
- and the act of sacrifice.

Their broken relationship is healed, and Esau calls Jacob "brother" (v. 9).

Equally full of twists and plots is the story of Joseph, the youngest son of Jacob. You may remember the story: Joseph was sold by his brothers into slavery, and his brothers told Jacob that Joseph was killed. Joseph went to Egypt and through a series of encounters with different people and interpreting their dreams, finally arrived in Pharaoh's court as a prominent man. A drought came to the land, but Joseph had prepared the land for the drought. As a result of the drought, Joseph's brothers went from Israel to Egypt to get food. Finally, Joseph revealed his identity to his family, and they were reconciled. Once again, the reconciliation was initiated by Joseph, the one who was wronged. He was willing to forgive his brothers and heal the broken relationship that had taken place years before. The depth of their reconciliation is reflected in Genesis 45:14–15, when, upon recognition they all embraced one another and wept.

The stories of Jacob, Esau, and Joseph are models of the ideal of God's forgiveness and the power of forgiveness to reconcile people to God and people to one another. The journey of forgiveness is played out before our eyes. It becomes apparent that forgiveness is an important factor in God's plan for us as human beings in the way we relate to one another and to God. It is important that we give proper attention to the place of forgiveness in our faith and in our lives.

## 1. Explore the scriptures

Review the two stories from Genesis (33:1–17; 45:1–15; 50:15–21), and the information in Before the Session.

Where do you see reconciliation in the story of Joseph and his brothers? If you were in Esau's position, how quickly would you have been able to forgive? If you were in Joseph's position, how quickly would you have been able to forgive?

## 2. Explore different levels of injury and pardon

Forgiveness is a journey that is easy or difficult depending on the people involved and the feelings surrounding the hurt or injury. *On the one hand,* we have experiences where a person has hurt us and we feel irritated or slighted but not devastated. Therefore, if the person apologizes, we can say, "I forgive you," or "I accept your apology." Perhaps the incident is not life changing. It is understandable to us that humans miscommunicate with each other or are unintentionally insensitive to one other. This type of wrong happens on a regular basis in most churches, families, and work places. If these slights and miscommunications are not dealt with in a timely fashion, the barrier between people will fester and grow. Later we may not even really remember what happened as much as we know that there is a barrier between us and the other person, a barrier that grows wider over time. The journey of forgiveness involves confrontation—confronting the pain, the injury, the barrier. While it is not easy, the journey of forgiveness will start by talking about the

Invite the group members to find the passages and read them silently. Then make or ask for a brief summary for each passage.

incident, each person accepting responsibility for their own part to the hurt, and the asking for forgiveness. It is much easier to confront the pain and instigate reconciliation early in a situation than to let it go and have to deal with a larger problem later. Practicing forgiving in small matters will enable us to handle forgiveness when larger matters arise.

*On the other hand,* we can be injured in ways that are life changing, hurt in ways that devastate us for a long period of time. Sometimes these injuries happened when we were children, and the rest of our lives were altered. Life-changing wrongs may have been brought about by people who meant well, but they made choices that were unwise. However, sometimes the wrongs were a continuing pattern that was perpetuated regardless of our needs. It is especially difficult when we were hurt by people we loved, by people whose job it was to care for us, nurture us, and protect us. Mixed feelings often make the process of forgiveness more stressed and the journey to reconciliation more rocky. (Is it healthy to accept an apology when we are still filled with rage and pain, and we doubt the other person's ability to truly understand the consequences of their behavior?)

Reflect on these questions and share your insights with the total group:

**Reflect and discuss.**

- Give examples of what kinds of injury might be easy to forgive, if the person who is asking is sincere.

- What are ways that the person accepting the apology expresses to the offender that forgiveness and reconciliation have taken place?

- Give examples of injuries where the ability to forgive might be extremely difficult. If the offender offers an apology insincerely or superficially, how does that impact the ability to forgive?

- What might be ways to respond to a person who asks for forgiveness without understanding the consequences of his or her behavior?

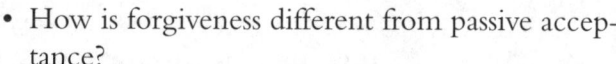

- How is forgiveness different from passive acceptance?

- How do we handle a situation where we are wronged and the other person is no longer available to be confronted?

- What do we do with unresolved pain? What part can forgiveness play in dealing with unresolved pain and injury?

### 3. Identify the steps of forgiveness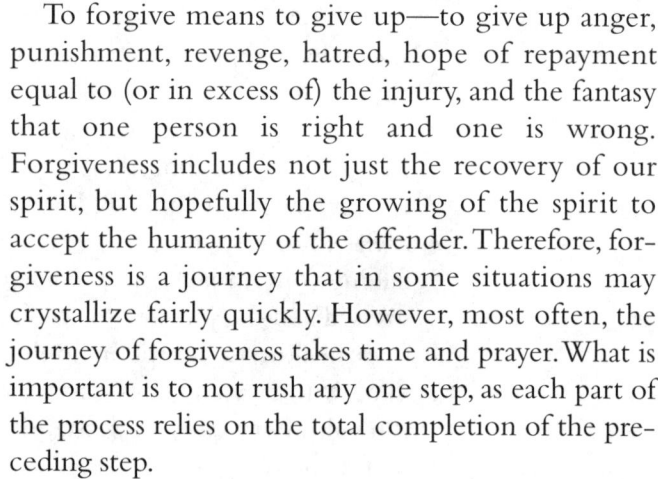

To forgive means to give up—to give up anger, punishment, revenge, hatred, hope of repayment equal to (or in excess of) the injury, and the fantasy that one person is right and one is wrong. Forgiveness includes not just the recovery of our spirit, but hopefully the growing of the spirit to accept the humanity of the offender. Therefore, forgiveness is a journey that in some situations may crystallize fairly quickly. However, most often, the journey of forgiveness takes time and prayer. What is important is to not rush any one step, as each part of the process relies on the total completion of the preceding step.

Consider times you feel you have completely forgiven someone in ways that led to healing and reconciliation. Looking back, what would you say were the steps you took? Can you describe the process (whether intentional or unintentional)?

The steps of the journey of forgiveness first begin with revisiting the incident. Forgiveness is not about stuffing feelings away or denying our pain. To revisit the injury needs to be a totally honest accounting of the situation. To revisit the injury is to express the anger, pain, and fear to a trusted person and become clearer about what causes us to feel as we do. This part of the journey may be a single episode of processing the pain, or it will be a conversation that happens as needed over an extended period of time.

CONNECTING WITH THE THEME

Review the steps. Write them on newsprint or a chalkboard and discuss each one.

Describe the process of forgiveness.

When a person has been abused (emotionally, physically, sexually, spiritually) they are frequently encouraged by others to "get over it" or "get past it." For someone who has been abused, the talking about and experiencing the pain are the first steps in claiming back their power and personal identity. This is the most-ignored step that when ignored, leads a person to remain stuck in the pain. How do you feel when someone wants to tell you details of a situation that has hurt her or him?

Secondly, an essential step in the journey of forgiveness is to acknowledge the humanity of ourselves and the offender. Blaming is not helpful. The natural tendency is to believe one person must be right, one must be wrong. This mind set is not helpful. Forgiveness is not necessarily about justice, it is about understanding that all people are children of God, but that we all sin and make mistakes. Accountability and blame are not the same. How are they different?

The third step is to confront the situation and confront the offender. This involves saying clearly and specifically what happened and the resulting consequences. For a person who has been abused, the identification of the abusive behavior and linking the consequences of that behavior to the pain is empowering and healing. Abuse happens in secret with distorted messages; to speak the truth is to break through the secretiveness and brings honesty to the feelings. Sometimes this is done in person, or in letter, or in writings that are later destroyed. Frequently it is wise to work through abuse with a professional therapist, especially if the goal is to confront the offender in person. Have you ever confronted someone who has seriously injured you?

Finally, letting go of the pain is the result of having dealt with the feelings, understanding our humanity, confronting the offender (or allowing the offender to come to us), and accepting the apology if it is open and sincere. How difficult is it for you to really let go of the pain? Can you identify your steps of being ready to let go?

### 4. Explore how you express forgiveness

**Help the group select partners, and set a time limit for the discussion. Choose a partner and share your own stories.**

Choose a partner from the group (preferably not a family member). Be attentive to the time so both people have an equal opportunity to share. Sit with your partner so that both can hear the other easily. Remind yourself that this sharing is confidential and that nothing you hear is to be repeated. Reflect quietly on the following and begin to discuss when both are ready:

*How do the steps just discussed agree or disagree with how you view the journey of forgiveness? If you are comfortable sharing, give an example of a hurt that you were able to forgive quickly. What is an example of an injury that required a long time to forgive (or that you are still working on) as you move toward forgiveness? How is God's timing integral in your journey of forgiveness? Are you able to identify your steps on the journey of forgiveness?*

### 5. Examine possible resolution in difficult situations

**Read and discuss. Invite people to offer examples of situations that are difficult to resolve, and what options might be open.**

What if the other person does not want my forgiveness? Does the other person need to say, "I am sorry"? The true reconciliation that comes when people acknowledge pain *and* offer apology is indeed healing and restoring. However, we may not have that option. It is frequently the person who has hurt us the deepest who refuses to talk, acknowledge the pain, or consider that forgiveness is necessary. This type of situation can make the journey of forgiveness more difficult.

What does a person do if the offender has died and the option of personal confrontation is not possible? Sometimes the person who hurt us so deeply lives elsewhere, and we have no idea where they live or even if they are alive. In other cases we cannot even be sure what happened to us because family and friends handle stress by keeping secrets. How do we offer forgiveness when we may not even have clarity about what we are forgiving?

A conflict is likely to arise when the person who hurt us is unavailable for the reconciliation process. This unavailability may be for one of a hundred reasons, but the fact remains that dealing directly with the person who wronged us is not an option. However, the pain is still inside us and may be causing problems with our relationships, our work situations, our ability to handle conflicts, our hopes and dreams, and our spirituality. What are our choices? Is our pain going to manage us, or are we going to manage our pain?

> What other examples can the group think of where long-term emotional burdens bring physical damage to a person?

To hold resentment and pain does damage to a person physically because feelings are not lost. If feelings are not faced, they will stay in the body and be expressed in unhealthy ways, such as headaches, stomach problems, or inappropriate behavior. Carrying devastation inside us can cause barriers to spiritual growth and healthy relationships. People who have been abused as children frequently have a higher risk for infection, accidents, broken bones, and a variety of medical concerns. Sometimes when a person begins to talk about traumatic events, they have a physical reaction that can make them sick enough to spend time in bed. Frequently the person has a physical response that is consistent with the original abuse. (Examples: If hit on the arms as a child, later, as an adult when discussing the abuse the arms may be painful to the point of almost being immovable. Females who have been raped may later experience specific pain consistent with the rape from years ago. Being in touch with anger now may cause headaches and body stress similar to the feelings at the time of the abuse that happened at a different point in time).

What are some ways that people in such situations can find healing? How can the church be a source of healing?

## 6. Decide personal responsibility

We are not responsible for abuse that happened to us by adults when we were children. However, we are responsible for how we handle our pain today. We are not responsible for unhappy family members who use alcohol and other drugs. However, we are responsible for our own choices about using alcohol and drugs. We are not responsible for being innocent victims in the past. We are responsible today for how we continue to put ourselves at risk of being victimized.

Discuss the following as a group. Remember that people will have different opinions depending on their own personal experiences. Accept the differences of opinion. Respect that people are impacted differently and grow in understanding and insight in different time frames.

*Discuss. Be sensitive to the differences in the group while discussing the questions.*

- How reasonable is it for a person to forgive when the offender is unavailable?
- What steps does a person take to reach being ready to forgive?
- Is the memory contained in the body really a serious problem? How does a person know if they have in fact "stuffed it" and are not aware of it?
- Is it healthy to intentionally forgive an offender who is unavailable so that the pain is released?
- How is prayer essential to the healing process when the offender is unavailable?

## 7. Read a psalm

Have a member of the group read Psalm 139:1–18. As the scripture is read have the group members reflect on what the scripture means to

**Explore the scriptures together.**

them. Is there a verse or set of verses that particularly speak to them personally? How could this psalm impact your everyday life? How does Psalm 139 relate to forgiveness?

## 8. Pray together 🔑

**Pray together.**

For the closing prayer, form a circle holding hands. Invite any members to offer a sentence prayer, if they wish. Then conclude the prayer time with Psalm 139:23–24:

*"Search me, O God, and know my heart; test me and know my thoughts. See if there is any wicked way in me, and lead me in the way everlasting."* Amen

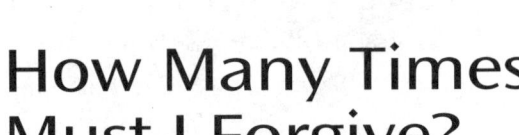

# 4

# How Many Times Must I Forgive?

*Session Focus: When faced with difficult situations, how do we offer forgiveness? How often should we forgive? What does Jesus say about offering forgiveness? Is it really a good idea to "forgive and forget"?*

Scriptures Used: Matthew 18:21–22; Psalm 32

BEFORE THE SESSION

Reflect on your previous definition of forgiveness. How is your understanding of forgiveness changing, growing?

One of the blocks to forgiveness is the belief that a person needs to forget when they forgive. Sometimes the internal pressure to forget weighs heavier than the pressure to forgive. If a person remembers the sin, does that mean a person has really forgiven another?

What is the benefit of forgetting the sin? What is the benefit of remembering what happened? One of the benefits of forgetting the sin is that this method makes moving past the incident so much easier. The belief is that by forgetting early, the pain will go away sooner. Do you believe this is accurate? In reality forgiveness happens at the end of the journey, not early in the process, so we cannot get around the pain. Rather, we must face it squarely.

Obviously "forgive and forget" is different based on each individual incident. If a person accidentally bumps me, I drop my groceries, and the offender is honestly sorry, then forgetting as well as forgiving is no problem. However, if a person has been abused, how do you forget that? It is not realistic or healthy to forget a seriously painful incident. Painful happenings so shape our lives and inform who we are at our core that to expect us to forget what happened makes no sense.

Encourage group members to give examples.

### 1. Ponder the concept of "forgive and forget"

Do you believe forgetting is essential to forgiveness? What incidents of injury to you have been easy to forget? difficult to forget? Do you think that "forgive and forget" is the agenda of the injured party or does it tend to be the agenda of the offender and/or people who are not part of the process? What have you been taught about forgetting when you forgive? Who taught you? What do you believe? What have you practiced in your life?

Reflect and discuss.

### 2. Consider the learning process of forgiveness

In a healthy journey of forgiveness, the person who was offended hopefully grows and learns from what happened to him or her. Life is a learning process, and to forget the sin implies that we do not need to learn from our life experiences. There is a difference between forgetting the sin and holding a grudge. When I hold a grudge and nurture resentment toward the offender, then I have not truly forgiven. When I continue to talk about and rehearse the injury to anyone who will listen, then I am not ready to forgive. The journey of forgiveness includes:

- moving through the pain
- processing what happened
- accepting any responsibility for any unhealthy participation in the injury

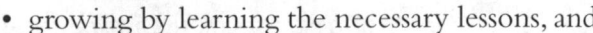

- growing by learning the necessary lessons, and
- forgiving the offender by taking steps to avoid a reoccurrence of the patterns connected to the injury.

What life lessons have you learned by the process of being hurt? How long did it take to learn the lesson? How have life lessons helped you clarify God's will for your life? How has forgiveness helped you stretch and grow?

### 3. Consider the importance of trust

*Discuss in small groups of two or three.*

Erik Erikson identified stages of human development through which each person progresses as they mature and grow. Each stage of development has a "task" upon which the person works. Further, he believes that each stage is only as strong as the preceding stage. This implies that these stages are developed much like building a brick wall where every new layer is placed on a previous layer that hopefully is sturdy. What do you think happens when a sturdy layer of bricks is placed on a layer of bricks that are cracked or defective? According to Erikson the beginning "task" for a person is trust versus mistrust. This is the earliest stage of development, and it begins in infancy. Therefore, the implication is that trust is the foundation upon which all the other stages are built. Also, trust is the basic foundation of all important and lasting relationships. Trust is not just one aspect of a relationship, it is the very basis upon which relationships grow.

The issue of trust has implications for the ability to give and receive forgiveness. If I trust someone and they make a mistake that does not affect my ability to trust that person, then reconciliation may seem hopeful. If I have trusted someone and do not believe they are capable of certain behaviors, and then that person makes a serious mistake, the core trust is shattered. One way to view it is to consider trust much like the foundation of a house. When the foundation has a major crack, repairing the damage may require total reconstruction.

Broken trust takes a long time to heal enough to be ready to consider forgiveness. It is possible to forgive when trust has been broken, but the injured person needs the time and space to work through the pain. More often than not, friends and family will push for forgiveness out of their own agenda and discomfort with the unresolved situation. Frequently, it takes courage to give oneself permission to take the time necessary to move past feelings, especially betrayal and rejection.

What role do you believe trust plays in forgiveness? How do you believe trust is rebuilt after it has been broken? Have you ever tried to forgive someone you did not trust? What happened?

Does the gospel ask us to be victims, to be assaulted over and over again? Some believe that forgiving "seven times seventy" means lack of boundaries and accepting inappropriate behavior time after time. Did Jesus model a "doormat" theology, or did he call people to accountability and responsibility?

## 4. Listen to the scriptures

> Read Matthew 18:21–22. Ask, "If you were one of the disciples, what question might you have asked Jesus after hearing these words?"

Earlier in Session 2, we discussed that Christians' forgiveness of others is founded on the fact that Christians themselves are forgiven. We forgive others because God has forgiven us. This model was on Peter's mind when he asked the question of Jesus, "Lord, if another member of the church sins against me, how often should I forgive?" (Matthew 18:21). Peter was aware of the Old Testament practice of forgiveness—you forgave three times. This concept came from the book of Amos beginning with the first chapter. Amos set a series of condemnations on various nations "for three transgressions and four," from which we deduce that God's forgiveness extended to three offenses, and that he visited the offender on the fourth with punishment.

So Peter was being quite benevolent when he suggested seven. He knew by now that Jesus' teaching went beyond and broadened the law. Jesus' answer, however, was seven times seventy. In other words, in Jesus' eyes there is no limit to forgiveness. When we put in perspective the length to which God went to forgive us, it makes sense that forgiveness is limitless. It is a reoccurring theme in the Gospel of Matthew to minister to "the least of these," generally meaning outcasts and sinners. It follows that if God forgives even "the least of these," how much more should we be willing to forgive others? *The Interpreter's Bible* commentary on verse 21 suggests that, "…this is celestial arithmetic: we must 'do it in our hearts.'"[1]

Forgiveness does not keep count. This sounds neither human nor possible. It is one of the most difficult of Jesus' sayings in this Gospel according to Matthew to consider. It is interesting that in Luke's Gospel after this saying of Jesus, the disciples respond, "increase our faith!" (Luke 17:5). The journey of forgiveness does not exist in a vacuum. It is a part of our greater journey of faith. We are humans, and as humans we do bear grudges; we carry our pain in scars that are slow to heal. Jesus knows that, and Jesus calls us to grow in our faith and ability and to practice forgiving others, as we ask forgiveness for ourselves.

## 5. Explore what the scripture means

In small groups of three or four members, consider the scripture telling us to forgive seven times seventy. What does this mean to you? What is Jesus teaching us about forgiveness? Each small group will write a consensus statement (one to two sentences) expressing the essence of this scripture passage. When finished, each group will read their statement to the whole group.

> Form teams for discussion. Make sure each has pen and paper. Have newsprint and markers ready.

Where are the statements similar? different? Combine the statements to make a composite statement. Print this on newsprint and post it or all to see.

## 6. Ponder the place of anger in forgiveness

Reflect and discuss.

The issue of anger presents an interesting dilemma. It is normal that the journey of forgiveness will involve feelings of resentment and anger, especially if the injury is serious. Frequently, the more serious the offense, the more angry and resentful the injured person will be. Therefore, time and a loving environment is beneficial as the hurt party faces and works through the pain. Anger is a part of the pain and should not be denied or ignored. God created us with feelings, and these feelings tell us when something is wrong, when a situation is dangerous, risky, or hurtful. We need to listen to our feelings but not be controlled by them.

Anger can serve a useful purpose for us. It gives us information. The first piece of information anger tells us is that there is something wrong. It provides an alarm system that alerts us to problems. The second piece of information anger tells us is that the person who has the anger owns the anger and with it the responsibility for dealing with the anger and for making changes. Our culture does not usually support this concept. I would like to believe that the other person makes me angry and thus my anger will only go away when the other person changes. Perhaps this is why authentic anger is such a struggle: The person with the anger is the only one who can choose how to handle it.

On the other hand, a person can use his or her anger to manipulate or control others. Anger can be used to punish the people who hurt us. Anger can be used to attract attention and elicit sympathy. Explore how you "use" anger. Are you able to control it? Do you express it in ways that are appropriate? A person can become stuck in anger, and this blocks the process. If a person feels stuck in anger and is not progressing, a question to ask is "What is the benefit of my holding on to anger?" Most people would respond that there is no benefit of having rage burn inside. What would cause a person to hang on to such incredibly painful feelings?

List any benefits of the decision to nurture anger. What are the possible benefits of being stuck? What are possible benefits of feeling trapped and powerless over resentment? How can family and friends unintentionally be encouraging someone to stay angry and resentful? How might being stuck in anger and fear of the future be connected?

### 7. Share themes and patterns

*Help the group form teams for discussion and set a time limit. Remember that what you hear is confidential, what you share is your choice.*

Talk with a group member (not a relative) about how you handle anger. What is your pattern of dealing with anger? Have there been times when you felt you would lose control over your anger? How do you handle anger as a part of the forgiveness process? Have you ever been stuck in the anger process? How did you get unstuck (or did you)?

### 8. Hear the word of God

*Reflect on your personal journey of learning to trust God and decide what part of your story to use in starting the discussion.*

Listen as a member of the group reads Psalm 32 aloud. The psalms were written by people like you and me who had encounters with God in their lives. They experienced all of the feelings delegated to humans. You do not have to look far in the psalms to find the four major feelings expressed that we humans experience: mad, sad, glad, and fearful. The author of Psalm 32, it is reasonable to believe, had experienced forgiveness and found that experience to bring joy. The author actually equates being forgiven as a blessing, being blessed. "Blessed are they whose transgressions are forgiven, whose sins are covered..." (Psalm 32:1). Have you ever been forgiven and felt that sense of joy, freedom and love all at the same time? Would you express it as did the psalmist, "Happy are those whose transgression is forgiven, whose sin is covered…"?

## 9. Learn about trusting God

> Have people select different partners than in previous activities.

Just as trust is the foundation of our earthly relationships, trust in God is our spiritual foundation. Faith is about our trust in God that grows continually through our entire lives. One way we build trust with God is by forgiving others and ourselves and allowing ourselves to accept God's forgiveness. To do so opens our souls to unlimited joy.

Discuss with a group partner your experience in trusting God. Is trusting God easy for you? difficult? Have you ever felt trust with God was broken? How was the foundation of trust restored? What have you learned about trusting God and the ways in which trust grows?

## 10. Identify joy in your life

After a few moments of quiet reflection each person in the group is asked to complete this sentence aloud, "What makes my heart jump for joy is…" The leader may then conclude the group with a prayer:

> *"Thank you God that abiding love surrounds those who trust in you. We rejoice in you and shout for joy for we are yours. Amen."*

---

[1] George Arthur Buttrick, ed., *The Interpreter's Bible,* vol. 7 (Abingdon, 1951).

# 5

# Must We *Always* Forgive?

*Session Focus: Sometimes we may separate from the situation rather than offer forgiveness. When is it appropriate to withhold forgiveness? How does accountability relate to when or if a person forgives?*

**Scriptures Used: Acts 15:36–40; Luke 17:3–5**

BEFORE THE SESSION

Reflect on the joy in your life that comes from trusting God.

CONNECTING WITH ONE ANOTHER

Acts 15:36–40 tells us part of a story of two committed Christians. Paul and Barnabas had a history together where they had worked as a team in ministry. Then they reached a point where a disagreement brought them to a crossroads. Surely this must have been a time of anguish and pain for them both. The end result of their difference of opinion was that they chose to part company and each follow their own conviction, even though it meant no longer working together. What can we learn from their example? How does one discern if more negotiation and compromise is needed or if it is time to agree to disagree which means breaking the relationship?

## 1. Listen to the pain of others

Relationships are hard work, and the breaking of relationships is deeply personal, a complex

*Discuss together and be careful not to judge.*

experience that has roots in the very core of who we are and how we see ourselves. To say to someone, "I know how you feel," is well intentioned but inaccurate. Everyone's pain is individual, even though the situations may be similar. Discuss together what situations cause feelings so painful that to say, "I know how you feel," is inaccurate and not helpful. Identify times in your life when you felt this way. What are some ways a person can offer love and support without trying to fix or minimize the pain of the person who is suffering?

## 2. Consider the lessons of history

History tells us that people are capable of inflicting incredible acts of pain and suffering. Most of us struggle to comprehend that such acts of inhumanity are even possible. Frequently we cannot bring ourselves to hear or read about acts in history because the pain of it all is upsetting and impossible to process.

*Read and discuss as a total group.*

A visit to the Holocaust Museum in Washington D.C. brings the visitor to the reality of what the victims experienced. The power of such knowledge frequently leaves the visitor with feelings and memories that produce sleepless nights, tears, and an overwhelming sense of grief and loss. Visitors to the museum may need a time of debriefing with a trusted person to even begin to process what they felt during the visit. To say, "Let's forgive and forget the Holocaust," is a denial of what actually took place during that time and the time since World War II ended. The world needs to fully understand the truth of the Holocaust in order to totally recommit that we will never allow such atrocities to happen again.

Extreme human abuse can be so painful that we want to minimize or avoid the truth of what happened. To do so discounts the pain of those who are victimized, denies their story that has changed their lives, and invalidates the severity of the abuse. While it is a human reaction to want to believe it is not that bad, to have that attitude can block the very healing of those injured. Healing happens when we face reality with those who have been abused and acknowledge that it *was* that bad, it never should have happened, and no one ever deserves such treatment.

### 3. Name the tragedy, face the reality

Discuss together as a group or in small groups of two or three.

The Holocaust is just one example of extreme cruelty in the world. What types of tragedies are so abhorrent to you that even to think about them brings pain? What situations of suffering when raised do you want to minimize or avoid? Considering the community where you live, what situations are of great concern? Do you tend to push uncomfortable thoughts and feelings out of your mind? How do you feel when you are upset or outraged at injustice, and others refuse to deal with you and/or your concerns?

### 4. Determine who "owns" the pain

Discuss.

In times of tragedy we need to remember who "owns" the pain. Whose pain is it? It is not unusual for those close to the situation who are not actually participants to want to try and fix the situation by offering forgiveness. However, the privilege of forgiving (or not forgiving) is the right of the people involved in the incident and pain itself.

I was not imprisoned by the Nazis. I was not one of the students shot in the cafeteria at Thurston High School in Springfield, Oregon. It was not my child who was killed by a drunk driver. Therefore, it is inappropriate and presumptuous of me to offer forgiveness and to pressure any person involved directly in such events to forgive the offender. The people directly victimized are the ones to own the right to forgive (or not) when the time is right for them. Do you agree or disagree? How might my pressuring a victim to forgive invalidate their experience? When have you ever had a person think you should forgive someone when you were not ready or interested in forgiving? How did being pressured make you feel?

> Can the group name other examples from the news?

An example of this situation occurred in a shooting incident at a Kentucky school. A disturbed student broke into the meeting of a student Bible study group and began firing, killing and wounding several youth. After the incident, members of the group held up signs where the killer could see them, saying "We forgive you." Some people questioned whether forgiveness was appropriate, without questioning their sincerity. Were the members of the student religious organization the ones to forgive? Did their forgiveness cheapen the grief and loss of the families? What would be your response if you were a member of that community? What role can churches play in working through community tragedies such as this?

## 5. Contrast nonabusive versus abusive treatment

The whole issue of forgiveness calls us to a deeper level of understanding of human behavior and to a clearer ability to discern what is really happening. In non abusive situations there can be pain because a person has been inconsiderate, irresponsible, insensitive, or just plain obnoxious. Forgiveness may be difficult but within reach when we acknowledge that mistakes and inappropriate behavior are part of what it is to be human. Sometimes forgiveness means restoring the relationship, sometimes it means letting go of the pain, wishing the other person well, and choosing to discontinue that relationship. Prayer gives us clarity and discernment about these painful situations.

Abusive situations require a different discernment and understanding. Abuse can be emotional, mental, spiritual, or physical. People who are being abused are frequently discounted, invalidated, controlled by intimidation and fear, and may have been physically battered. People who abuse tend to rationalize to themselves and others that what they are doing is justified, that their behavior is explainable. Abusive people tend to have what counselors call "thinking errors," meaning that their basic thinking process is distorted and inaccurate. However, people who are abusive will defend their thinking process and actions because it makes perfect sense to them. (Example: "I had to hit my children because their behavior required that response.")

The issue around forgiving an abusive person is clouded by the fact that the abuser may not process the meaning of forgiveness in the same way as the person offering the forgiveness. On psychiatric units where residents are dealing with inappropriate, abusive behavior, the therapy staff may resist having the residents visited by a minister or church members. Why? Because if the Christian visitor tells the resident that God forgives them, the resident will frequently translate that to mean, "What I did is not that serious. I am forgiven; I can do it again." Recovery for a person relies heavily on guilt as a motivation. Premature forgiveness erases the guilt and the person is thus free to reoffend.

Talk together about the difference between abusive and nonabusive behavior. Both can be hurtful; however, the intent, motivation, consequences, and impact may be different. Different in what ways? What are characteristics common to nonabusive situations where people might feel hurt, offended, abandoned, or rejected? What are characteristics of abusive behavior that may be subtle and difficult to identify? What are characteristics of abusive behavior that tend to be overt?

### 6. Contrast blame and accountability

As humans beings we can easily proceed to blaming people other than ourselves if we are hurt. This is

> As a group, define abusive versus nonabusive behavior. What are some examples of each?

especially true if we tend to think in terms of black and white, meaning that one of us is wrong and one of us is right. I'm sure that I'm right, so it must be your fault. Frequently the truth is somewhere in between—for instance, we both contribute to the misunderstanding, or we both participated in inappropriate behavior. Blame is a fruitless adventure that keeps people stuck and blocks healing.

*Ponder characteristics of blame and accountability.*

On the other hand, accountability is another issue. Jesus regularly called people to accountability that included thoughts and feelings as well as behavior. People who are abusive must be held accountable in order to repent, heal, and make amends.

If I were abused as a child, and I went to confront my parents, am I blaming or asking for accountability? If I am late to a meeting, and I explain my husband did not wake me on time, am I blaming or explaining accountability? If I drank too much because my job is stressful, am I blaming or am I saying that my boss is accountable for my pain? Share together the definition of blaming versus accountability and give examples.

## 7. Examine abuse in families

*Discuss as a group or in teams of three or four.*

A situation our communities face every day is the issue of domestic violence. A person who abuses in this situation, because of errors in their thinking may actually express remorse. Usually the "I am sorry" is about being sorry for being caught, or for the consequences of the abuse, but not sorrow for the abuse itself. Once a partner offers forgiveness, it releases the offender to continue the abuse. Churches may encourage the hurt partner to forgive, not understanding that to do so may increase rather than decrease the risk of further abuse. How does one determine whether forgiveness will bring about healthy reconciliation, or will it actually escalate the abuse cycle?

*Must We Always Forgive?*

Forgiveness is appropriate only after the offenders have changed their behavior for an extended amount of time. Usually this means completion of a counseling or treatment program. It is common for the family to see changed behavior for one or two weeks and believe forgiveness is in order. Actually this may be the "honeymoon" phase before the abuse begins again. Changed behavior consistent over time requires correcting the thinking errors that can only happen over months or years of therapy.

Frequently a battered partner will say, "My spouse became drunk, verbally abused me, and physically assaulted me. My spouse cried today, apologized, and promised never to behave that way again. Shouldn't I accept the apology?" The correct answer is yes, of course, accept an apology. But be sure it's *after* that person has had a full alcohol and drug evaluation, successfully completed a treatment program, completed a year of aftercare, has a sponsor while working a 12-step program, has accepted full responsibility for inappropriate behavior with no excuses, and makes full amends, including financial compensation. Then, if you are ready to forgive and it is what you choose (not what you think you should do), then forgive. Is this situation about blame or accountability? What is most likely to happen if people who batter are forgiven every time they say they are sorry?

Reflect: What are ways that your church or the churches in your community can offer a haven for people who are abused?

## 8. Consider the issue of safety

During the recovery process, the person who was abused needs also to learn self-care and self-protection, which means separation from the person who offended. Safety is a priority that needs to be honored. To put oneself in danger does not honor God. To ask a person to be at risk to avoid upsetting an abusive family member is not consistent with the intent of the gospel. Self-care is not selfish when it comes to being at risk or in danger. An abusive person does not change or grow when others feel self-care is selfish.

It can be difficult for Christians to understand that walking away may be, in some situations, the healthiest for all involved. Some people are unhealthy to the point of putting the people around them at risk. People are very different in personality and some personalities are so opposite that it is unrealistic to push for a workable relationship. Some people are just plain toxic to one another. Although both people may be well-meaning, no one understands why the relationship is toxic. God calls us to discern what is and is not possible in creating healthy relationships. Occasionally discernment tells us to emotionally wish a person well and go our separate ways.

## 9. Look at the reality of repentance

*Discuss. Give examples.*

In an ideal world the person causing pain says, "I'm sorry," forgiveness is offered, and reconciliation takes place. However, the offender may not ask for forgiveness, or, in fact, be sorry or acknowledge there is a problem with his or her behavior. Now what?

Prayer and discernment may bring the injured person to separate from the offender. Sometimes this is necessary for emotional stability and self-care. If the behavior is abusive, and the offender refuses to understand how inappropriate the situation is, the person who is hurt may choose to break the relationship. It is impossible to fix a serious problem when one of the participants refuses to see that a problem exists.

Sometimes we forgive someone as a personal, internal process for our own emotional and spiritual health, but we do not offer forgiveness to the offender. To do so would, at times, cause more harm than good.

Accountability is essential to the healing process. Trying to forgive and/or reconcile with a person who refuses to be accountable or accept responsibility is like trying to nail Jell-O to a wall. So the conclusion might be to internally and privately forgive a person for your own mental and spiritual health and go your separate way.

Do you believe that in some situations a person's healthiest response is to separate from the relationship? Give some examples of when this might be necessary. How can one person make another person accept responsibility? When might people work on their own issues, release the pain, and go on with their lives, accepting the fact that reconciliation is inappropriate or impossible?

## 10. Hear the word of God

*Ask a member of the group to read aloud Luke 17:3–5.*

Talk together about the implications of Luke's retelling of how many times Jesus said to forgive. Does this seem harsh to you? How does this passage connect with what we have been discussing in this session? How does this passage relate to accountability? How does this passage apply to our daily lives?

As time allows, look again at the story of Paul and Barnabas as discussed in Before the Session (Acts 15:36–40). What wisdom do you see in their mutual decision to part ways? How does it show us the humanity of Christian leaders? What does it show us about moving past a disagreement and getting on with our lives?

## 11. Pray together

*You may want to light a candle as a sign of God's light during the closing prayer time.*

Life is not black and white. Answers are not always easy and clear. Situations vary and people are individuals, therefore a rule that applies in one situation does not necessarily fit another situation. That is why prayer and discernment are essential. The more we trust God and ask for clarity, the better discernment skills we develop.

Commit yourself, during the week ahead, to pray for discernment each day to help you face the conflicts and uncertainties that the day brings.

Join hands and pray together. Each person who chooses so will complete the sentence, "God I ask discernment for..." The whole group will respond, "Hear our prayer" after each sentence prayer. After all who choose to share have done so, the leader will close with a benediction.

# 6

# Does Forgiveness Involve More than Just Me and the Other Person?

*Session Focus: Forgiveness goes beyond the sins of individual people. Does a whole community, nation, or specific group of people need forgiveness? Who calls them to forgiveness? Is there such a case as sins of omission? If a nation or group sins and seeks forgiveness, how do they find it? Who affirms it? How do they know they are forgiven?*

Scriptures Used: Hosea 14:4–7; Joel 2:12–22

BEFORE THE SESSION

In preparation for this session, read the opening paragraphs and reflect on the role forgiveness plays in relationships between groups in society.

I remember as a child in the fifth grade how a plan spread through the students during recess one day. At exactly 2:15 that afternoon, all the students in the two fifth grade classes would drop all their pencils on the floor at the same time. It was intended as a joke. The little joke sounded harmless and fun. Our teacher, a wonderful teacher whom I adored, was in the middle of giving a lesson. Suddenly, at the appointed hour, the majority of students dropped their pencils, and the noise of all those pencils dropping was thunderous. Our teacher responded first with a look of shock and then put her head on her desk and sobbed. It hurt her feelings deeply. The next day, each pupil who had participated had to face the teacher for punishment. I had to write a ten-page report. When all the students had completed their assignments, our teacher gave each person a pencil as a peace offering. I kept that pencil for years as a reminder of that time of guilt and forgiveness.

That act of hurting and forgiveness involved a group of people. It was more than one-on-one. We are part of many communities, and the actions—be they hurtful or reconciling—that make up community life go beyond individual actions. From classroom to workplace, from neighborhood to nation, we experience (and pass on) corporate pain and hurt. We as individuals and communities then have to make decisions about forgiveness. How do the dynamics of forgiveness work in a larger setting? Think about it and pray about it as you prepare for this session.

## 1. Pray together

Look through the section together, and pray together the Lord's Prayer, using the emphasis found here.

During much of this study, we have been considering forgiveness as part of an individual's relationship to another person, or an individual's relationship with God. However, we are not isolated individuals. Our relationships with others and our relationship with God is a part of a larger set of relationships. We are part of communities, and these communities help define us and set the context for the way we act, think, feel, worship, and even forgive. This session will help us see some of the larger dimensions of forgiveness.

When Jesus taught the disciples to pray, he did not ask them to pray for their own individual needs, but to pray as part of a community of God's children. The words of the Lord's Prayer are very familiar. Many of us recite them every Sunday during worship. Pray the words again, together as a group.

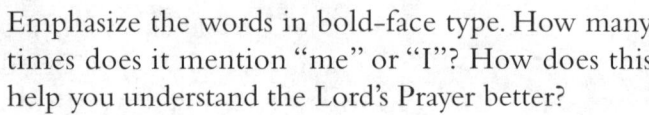

Emphasize the words in bold-face type. How many times does it mention "me" or "I"? How does this help you understand the Lord's Prayer better?

**Our** Father in heaven,
    Hallowed be your name.
    Your kingdom come,
    Your will be done,
        on earth as it is in heaven.
    Give **us** this day **our** daily bread.
    And forgive **us our** debts,
        as **we** forgive **our** debtors.
    And do not bring **us** to the time of trial,
        but rescue **us** from evil.
For the kingdom and the power and the glory are yours forever. Amen.
(Matthew 6:9b–13, alternate readings)

## 2. Recall your community

> Invite someone to keep a group list on newsprint or chalkboard. Help the group identify similarities and differences among the organizations.

How many different groups do you belong to? How many have you belonged to in your life? Sunday school class, Boy Scouts, Girl Scouts, swim team, Spanish club, bike club, aerobics class, Rotary, Kiwanis, auxiliary, professional organizations, secret societies, a group of friends, book study group, church, denomination, service organization, neighborhood association, a clan, nationality, or unique family—all these are just a few examples. List as many as you can. Share your list with others in the group, see what similarities you share and what differences you can find. Maybe someone else's list will jog your memory. You can add any you forgot. You may be surprised at the number of groups to which you have belonged.

## 3. Recall a community at risk

> If there are more than eight in the group, form teams of three or four

Now think of a time when a group you belonged to made a mistake, a poor judgement, or acted in a way that brought hurt to others. If you cannot recall a group you have belonged to that has been in this *to discuss the questions, then have the teams summarize their discoveries to the whole group.*

situation, recall a situation where some other group had such a difficulty.

How did it feel to be in a whole group that faced this dilemma? Did you know at the time you were participating in something that was wrong? Who blew the whistle on the action? How did it stop? What were the consequences? Who was hurt? Tell some of these stories within your group.

### 4. Recall the community forgiveness

*Read, reflect, and discuss with one another in the group or in the teams formed in activity 2. You will want to make sure that group members have pencil and paper available to record their thoughts and responses.*

Reflect on the group you were a part of that created a difficult situation. Many groups have rules or bylaws that specifically map out the consequences of misbehavior and of correcting the situation through discipline or discharging of members. How did the group(s) of which you were a member deal with the wrong? Was the total group chastised or penalized for its action? Who offered the forgiveness? How did you know when the forgiveness was complete? How did you feel when the situation was resolved? Once again, share your feelings with the group or team. As you share and listen to the other members of the group, listen for ways that forgiveness can be offered in these instances.

### 5. Read Hosea 4:4–14

*Be ready to help people find the book of Hosea. Discuss.*

The history of God's relationship to the people in Old Testament times is a story of faithfulness and betrayal, successes and shortcomings, and ultimately the story of a nation in covenant with God. In many of the stories, God rewarded a single person's faithfulness in continuing to affirm God's presence and salvation—not just with that person but with a group of people, a clan, a community, a nation. And as the story of God building that nation unfolds, it includes times of sin and turning away from God, as well as times of faithfulness and growth that lead to God's forgiveness. However, the focus of the Old

Testament is the unfolding story of the life of Israel and Israel's relationship with God. The concept of forgiveness becomes a community issue, not just an individual issue. The prophets were God's spokespersons to the people. At times they served as the people's conscience; at other times they predicted God's actions of wrath or discipline. In all cases, they called the community to be faithful to its covenant with God. In the case of Hosea, he compared Israel's broken relationship to God with the relationship he had with his wife, who was a harlot (Hosea 3:1–5). God's forgiveness comes when not just one person, but the whole nation has a change of heart, repents, and enacts a new pattern of behavior. As a group, read Hosea 4:4–14. Discuss what you understand to be Israel's sin as a whole people, a community. What was their sin according to verse 6? How is God's forgiveness described in this passage (or is it)?

### 6. Read Joel 2:12–22

> Split the scripture into three or four parts according to the size of the group. Form teams of two or three. Assign groups sections of the scripture. It falls into four natural parts: Joel 2:12–14; 15–16; 17–19; 20–22. Ask each group to answer the questions and record their responses on paper to share with the total group.

In the Old Testament, God offers the people different ways to show that they seek and desire God's forgiveness. In some places it calls for sacrifice or a new form of behavior; in other places, something quite different is expected or offered. Also, God tells the people what will happen because of God's forgiveness. The passage in Joel records several different ways God tells of forgiveness. What do you think the particular sin or wrongdoing is in each section of the passage? What does God ask of the people in those situations? What will God do if they follow God's prescription for forgiveness? When (if ever) have you felt God's presence in any of these ways? How have those times been connected to the forgiveness of an act of wrongdoing by yourself or a group in which you have been a member?

### 7. Consider a case study

Consider a story of forgiveness in a setting of two cultures. On October 5, 1997, two different worlds

Have someone read the story aloud. Reflect on it in silence for a few moments. Then discuss the questions at the end.

collided when a young twenty-year-old man slammed his car into a horse-drawn buggy as a Mennonite family was on their way to church. This incident took place on a stretch of highway by a small town in Iowa, near where a group of fifty-two Mennonite families had settled to farm. This particular Mennonite family consisted of the thirty-year-old father, the mother, two boys, and three girls, one of which was an eight-month-old infant. As a result of the accident, the oldest girl, age seven, died, the infant was left blind and with brain damage, and it took months for the others to recover. The young man driving the car was not injured. The young man had been at a party where there was drinking.

Even before the smoke cleared from the wreckage, the Mennonite father forgave whoever had been behind the steering wheel of the car. "Behold, I send you forth as sheep in the midst of wolves: be ye therefore wise as serpents and harmless as doves" (Matthew 10:16, KJV) went through the father's head. When the little girl died in the hospital, the charges to the young driver of the car were changed to vehicular homicide. Yet the Mennonite father forgave the young man. The young man attended the funeral of the little girl. He also helped around the Mennonite family's farm while they were recuperating from the accident. The state filed charges against the young man. Yet he found some comfort in the Mennonite family's forgiveness.[1] Later, when the case came to trial, the jury found the driver guilty of vehicular homicide. Some of the family's spirit of forgiveness may have passed on to the judge and jury. The young man could have spent twenty-five years in prison. Instead, he had to pay the family a large amount in restitution and was sentenced to five years probation, one year to be spent in a residential facility. At the sentencing, the young man expressed his sorrow and sense of accountability, and that the memory of Katy, the girl who died, would be with him forever. A minister in the Mennonite community expressed the community's satisfaction at the sentence, saying that prison would not have helped the situation. The father of the dead child had no anger for the young man, only sorrow that the accident had to happen.[2]

If you were in the young father's shoes, could you so readily forgive the driver of the car? If you were the driver, how would you feel to know you were forgiven by the family? Have you ever been in a situation like this? How was or is forgiveness a part of the situation? Is it easy or difficult?

## 8. Ask for forgiveness

History is full of incidents where large groups of people have caused devastation to individuals or other large groups of people. We can name a few, such as the Egyptians to the Israelites in the time of Moses, or the Spaniards to the Aztecs in the colonization of Latin America. But we can also recall the same kind of atrocities in North American history, slavery with Africans, taking land from the Native Americans, or the internment camps for the Japanese Americans during World War II. Of course, there are others.

What about sins of omission? Those are times when we can act to stop a wrong, but we choose to stand by and watch, or worse yet, turn our backs and let it happen. As a nation we have sometimes let actions happen that have had devastating effects on others and not stepped in to act. What situations can you think of where this has happened or is happening? What situations can you think of today where this is happening in our own nation? What about abuses to our environment? What about racial prejudice that is still practiced today? How can we make restitution for dropping the atomic bomb on Japan? How can we rectify our actions toward countries in

> Be careful not to get sidetracked into political arguments about various policies and actions.

the Middle East that we bomb? How do we ask for forgiveness and show that we have repented? How are we as individuals part of the problem? part of the solution?

## 9. Decide about global forgiveness

Read the following information, then break into two groups and assign the groups to discuss one of the options below about genuine forgiveness. Come back as a total group and have each group report the results of their discussion.

The author, Walter Wink, in the article "Excuse Me" (*Christian Century*, October 21, 1998, 956–957) has this observation about our present day society:

> *The extension of apologies from persons to entire nations is one of the great innovations in statecraft in our time. It is as if the gospel imperative of reconciliation is being secularized and broadened to take in the collective life of entire peoples. The apology of one person to another, or of the one to many, has been extended to include the apology of the many to the one and the many to the many—even of one nation to another.*

He goes on to elaborate:

> *But not all apologies can be accepted. The U.S. bombardier who dropped an atomic bomb on Nagasaki offered to attend the fortieth anniversary commemoration and tender a public apology to the city. The offer was refused by city officers. The bomb killed an estimated 70,000 people and devastated the city. "We understand his sentiments, but there are many atomic bomb victims who are still suffering and who do not wish to meet this man," said a city official.*

Wink cites the fact that offering these kinds of apologies, for large historic atrocities, is a new phenomenon. Although they may not be accepted, he points out that it is important to offer them. He also differentiates between genuine apologies and apologies that are not genuine. The cases he points out that are genuine are situations where restitution, change of behavior, or change of attitude is affected.

Apologies that are not genuine are ones where there are words of repentance, but no change affected as a result. How would you judge the following two situations as to the presence of genuine forgiveness?

1. In 1976, the U.S. government apologized to the American citizens of Japanese descent who endured the internment camps of World War II. It took twelve years longer for Congress to authorized payments of $20,000 each to the internees who were still alive, and it took two years after that before the checks were issued. Is this a genuine offer of apology? Why or why not?

2. The United Church of Canada made a formal apology to the native people of Canada. The church apologized for imposing "our civilization on you as a condition for accepting our gospel." Is this a genuine offer of apology? Why or why not?

## 10. Ponder God's forgiveness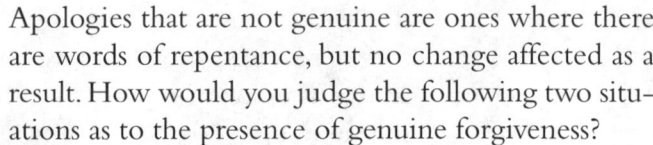

*Reflect and discuss.*

God called a group of people, the Israelites, into existence to be the model of how a relationship with God is supposed to work. That same nation fell out of favor with God on several occasions, occasions that called for repentance, discipline or punishment, and God's intervention. However, God offered forgiveness to that nation when it admitted its guilt and changed its behavior. Concerning our modern day, are there groups that God calls to repentance? What are some groups you can think of that need repentance and forgiveness? To what groups does God offer forgiveness today?

## 11. Think about the church and forgiveness

*Reflect and discuss.*

When does the church need to seek forgiveness? What actions or attitudes exist in the church that need to be explored, changed, or forgiven? On the other hand, what does the church need to forgive? Does the church have the right to "hand out" forgiveness? What scriptures do you have in mind to support your thoughts? Can you find them or quote them? Have you ever had a problem with the church? Have you ever felt forgiven in the church? Have you had to forgive others in church? How is or isn't the church a forgiving place?

In one congregation, the same man had been treasurer for many years. Whenever anyone suggested an audit of the books, the treasurer would get defensive and angry. Eventually, people stopped suggesting an audit. Finally, because of finding serious difficulties in the financial reports, the board chair ordered an audit. From the audit came evidence that the treasurer had embezzled thousands of dollars over several years.

What should they do? They confronted the treasurer with the evidence. This was difficult, because close bonds of friendship existed among the leaders of the congregation. He confessed to the embezzling, which he had done because his own family's financial situation had spun out of control. He was trying to avoid bankruptcy. The treasurer realized that he had committed a crime, acknowledged that the congregation had a right to press charges, and send him to prison. He stated that he would make restitution for all he had taken. He asked for their forgiveness.

> The group can either discuss or role-play the situation where the congregation's leaders had to decide what course of action to take. To discover what really happened, turn to p. 78 in Enriching the Experience.

What would you do if you were one of the congregation's officers or pastor? What factors would you take into account in guiding your choice?

### 12. Write a prayer list

Write down three incidents of community strife or conflict (local, national, or international) that you feel need God's intervention and forgiveness. Fold your piece of paper and place it on the floor in the

**CONNECTING WITH GOD**

Assure the group that the papers used in closing will be handled with confidentiality and destroyed, which is part of their offering to God.

middle of the group, along with papers from the other group members. Form a circle joining hands and have a time of silence for individual reflection and prayer. Then, with the group leader beginning, group members who want to can give spoken prayers for God's forgiveness in situations that are of concern to the group. The leader or the whole group in unison may then close this time with part of the assigned scripture from Joel:

> *Yet even now, says the LORD,*
>     *return to me with all your heart,*
> *with fasting, with weeping, and with mourning;*
>     *rend your hearts and not your clothing.*
> *Return to the LORD, your God,*
>     *for he is gracious and merciful,*
> *slow to anger, and abounding in steadfast love,*
>     *and relents from punishing. (2:12–13)*

Finish by saying the Lord's Prayer as a group.

---

[1] Des Moines Sunday Register, May 3, 1998, 4A.
[2] Des Moines Register, January 6, 1999, 1a, 4a.

# JOURNAL

# ENRICHING THE EXPERIENCE

Use the following activities during the six regular sessions, or during one or more special sessions.

## 1. Practice role-playing

Role-play incidents of accountability and the acts of asking for forgiveness. Decide together on some sample role-plays to try, perhaps based upon the situations for discussion. Role-play having a person accept an apology. Role-play a person offering an apology that is not accepted. Process the role-plays together by discussing both the ideas and feelings that came out.

## 2. Write letters

Write a letter to someone who has hurt you, where, for whatever reason, the person is not available to personally talk it through with you. In the letter, accept responsibility for any part of the problem in which you acted in an inappropriate or unhealthy way. Identify the part of the problem that belongs to the receiver of the problem. Make appropriate statements of asking for forgiveness or offering forgiveness. Bring the letters to worship time and offer prayers for the letter writers. Have a time when the letters are blessed, then burned or destroyed, and prayers for letting go are given.

## 3. Choose prayer partners

Each person in the group can choose a partner. Form groups of two. Each person will identify a specific issue around forgiveness upon which he or she wants to work. It may be a specific situation or one part of the process: For example, "I want to work on how to express regret to a family member," or "I have trouble getting past my anger, I want to work on feeling the anger and then releasing it." Each partner covenants to pray for the other every day. In a set amount of time (whatever the partners decide) the two will connect with each other to share how they are proceeding with their goals.

## 4. Worship together

Present this option to the congregation's leadership. Work together as a group to create a brief presentation on forgiveness that can be offered in a worship service. This can include such acts of worship as writing a litany, a prayer, or a verse to a favorite hymn tune. Or the group may want to develop and lead an entire worship service. Or the group may want to create and perform a skit or drama for settings such as a potluck supper, Sunday school, youth group, vacation Bible school, and so on.

## 5. Look at church history

Look at the history of your congregation or denomination. Being sensitive about confidentiality and being nonjudgmental, identify incidents in the church's history that were affected by people's inability to work out conflicts or to give and receive forgiveness. Each group member will take home a list of these painful incidents and pray daily for insight and discernment regarding these situations. Come together again at a different time (one-to-two weeks later), and share what you have learned during the prayer time. What thoughts did the prayers bring? What feelings arose from the prayers? What can you do as a group or an individual to help ease the pain or foster forgiveness in these situations? What can you as a group or individual do to create an environment in the church that might prevent these situations from reoccurring?

## 6. Create a banner

Have the group together create a banner on forgiveness that can be used in the sanctuary for worship.

## 7. Use art skills

Design a bulletin cover on forgiveness that can be used for worship, or artwork for church newsletter.

## 8. Teach God's forgiveness to children

If the group members are parents or grandparents of young or elementary-aged children, read and discuss the article "Teach Your Children about a Forgiving God" reprinted on p. 10. It is taken from Delia Halverson's book *How Do Our Children Grow?* (Chalice Press, 1999). What suggestions seem most appropriate? Create a plan to implement them. Plan a time that you can meet again to offer and receive feedback on your teaching experiences.

## What did they do?

(Answer to the situation described on p. 73.)

In this instance, the other leaders extended forgiveness, decided not to press charges, and accepted a plan of restitution. Then, as an expression of trust and forgiveness, they asked him to continue as treasurer. In other situations that would have been an inappropriate course of action. In this particular situation, the offender proved worthy of the trust the others placed in him.

# Building foundations for faithfulness

**HOW DO OUR CHILDREN GROW?**
**Introducing Children to God, Jesus, the Bible, Prayer, Church**
**Revised Edition**
*by Delia Halverson*

In an update of a popular resource, Halverson offers parents, caregivers, and educators solid, practical ways to introduce children and young people to the Christian faith.

Supplementing practical advice with concrete illustrations, she shows how to build the early foundations for faithfulness, introducing:

- God
- Jesus
- The Holy Spirit
- The Bible
- Prayer
- Death and Heaven
- Personal Mission
- Living Faithfully in Today's World

A study guide helps small groups and individuals make the most of the book's practical wisdom. 08272-14375, $14.99

*Delia Halverson* is an author and Christian education specialist who leads workshops for parents and teachers throughout the United States.

**Coming in October from Delia Halverson:**
*The Gift of Hospitality: In Church, in the Home, in All of Life*
08272-12437, $12.99

**Order from  Christian Board of Publication • 1-800-366-3383**
Box 179 • St. Louis, MO 63166-0179 • 314-231-8500 • Fax 314-231-8524
E-mail customerservice@cbp21 • Visit our Web site at www.cbp21.com

# LOOK FOR THESE FAITH CROSSINGS TITLES:

### Available now:

*God's Ordinary People*—A look at some fascinating but little-known biblical characters.

*Faith Talk*—An introduction to basic Christian beliefs.

*Following God into the Future*—As we welcome a new millennium, where will our faith journeys take us?

*Through the Fire*—A Bible study on facing tough times.

*ABC's of the Bible*—Twenty-six key verses draw us into the fascinating world of scripture.

*Show No Partiality*—A lively dialogue on facing the challenge of racism.

*Living Water*—Take the plunge! Explore the rich symbolism of water in the Bible.

*Worship—Whys, Whats, and Hows*—Explore what it means to worship God.

*Forgiveness—Who Needs It?*—In a complex and violent world, where does forgiveness fit in?

### Available December 1999:

*Talking Faith and Politics*—Never discuss religion and politics? This course takes on both!

*Who Is This Jesus?*—What does it mean to say that Jesus is the Christ?

*The Jesus Attitudes*—Are the Beatitudes pious notions or calls to radical discipleship?